Whispers of the Biafran Skeleton

also by Ngozi Olivia Osuoha

The Transformation Train
Letter to My Unborn
Sensation
Tropical Escape (with Amos O. Ojwang')
Fruits from the Poetry Planet
Poetic Grenade
Chains
Raindrops
Freeborn
Eclipse of Tides

Whispers of the Biafran Skeleton

poems by
Ngozi Olivia Osuoha

Poetic Justice Books & Arts
Port Saint Lucie, Florida

©2019 Ngozi Olivia Osuoha

book design and layout: SpiNDec, Port Saint Lucie, FL
cover design: Kris Haggblom
cover text: *The Ahiara Declaration: The Principles of the Biafran Revolution*, Colonel Chukwuemeka Odumegwu Ojukwu
cover image: *El genocidio de Biafra*, 1969, Camera Press-Zardoya

All rights reserved.

No part of this book may be used or reproduced in any manner whatsoever without written permission except in the case of brief quotations embodied in critical articles and reviews. Members of educational institutions and organizations wishing to photocopy any of the work for classroom use, or authors, artists and publishers who would like to obtain permission for any material in the work, should contact the publisher.

Published by Poetic Justice Books
Port Saint Lucie, Florida
www.poeticjusticebooks.com

ISBN: 978-1-950433-13-1

10 9 8 7 6 5 4 3 2

*This poetry book is dedicated to my father,
Mr. B. A. Osuoha, a Biafran veteran.*

table of contents

WAR 3
BOMB 4
PROPAGANDA 5
RAPE 6
AMMUNITION 7
HUNGER 8
TRENCHES 9
UNIFORM 10
MARGINALIZATION 11
DEATHS 12
BRIDGE 13
REFINERY 14
WAR MUSEUM 15
EVACUATION 16
ONE MAN ONE BULLET 17
ABDUCTION 18
LOOTS 19
BLOCKADE 20
THINGS FELL APART 21
CAPTURED 22
ENEMY 23
TRIBALISM 24
NO VICTOR 25
NO VANQUISHED 26
NO VICTOR NO VANQUISHED 27
FREEDOM 28
WAR SONGS 29
DESTRUCTION 30
GENOCIDE 31
MASS GRAVES 32
CONSCRIPTION 33
POWER TUSSLE 34
BUSINESS 35
TRAPS 36

DEFENSE	37
LOST	38
OJUKWU	39
DAD	40
AMALGAMATION	41
TONGUES AND TRIBES	42
EXILE	43
REFUGEES	44
MONEY	45
BURIAL RITES	46
BIGHT OF BIAFRA	47
SHADOWS	48
SKELETONS	49
LORRIES	50
AHBURI ACCORD	51
AHIARA DECLARATION	52
INJUSTICE	54
1967-1970	55
MILITARY HOSPITALS	56
GREED	57
VITAL POSITIONS	58
TODAY	60
PATRIOTISM	61
LOSSES	62
AMBUSHED	63
FRUSTRATIONS	64
THE STRUGGLE	66
BIAFRA	67
ATROCITIES	68
MILLIONS OF BIAFRANS	69
LEADERSHIP	70
FAULTY FOUNDATION	71
AGUIYI IRONSI	72

Whispers
of the
Biafran Skeleton

WAR

The corruptible judge
Sentencing young and old
Killing men, women and children
Dancing with skulls
And merrying with skeletons.

War, the priest of death
The warrior of inferno
The angel of doom
The demon of destruction,
War, the cycle of rituals.

War, respecter of none
Killer of any
Sweeper of good
Planter of evil.

War, saint of rivals
Bet of rivalry
Belt of powers
Shower of darkness,
Giver of sourness.

BOMB

Sounds of death, thundering
Thousands of breath, ceasing
Lands and climes, sinking
Millions of wealth, burning.

Bombs, bombs, bombs
Bombers and suicide bombers
Killers in red lines
Chasing lives, terminating nations
Bombs, bombs everywhere.

Enemies are bombing
Bombed, enemies
Casualties, destructions
Terrorism captured, losing
Bombs, wars, terrors.

PROPAGANDA

Propagandas cooking and smelling
Propagandists gaining, deceiving
Outsiders believed, doubtful
Fears, tears, confusion.

Deceit at its peak
Lies, false claims, illegalities
Hoping against hope
Deterring, defaming, deforming
Insiders concocting, compounding.

Propagandas monitoring, piling
Left, right, front, back, center
News, stories, gossip, scandals
Turmoils, echoes boiling
Reality eluding, losses building.

RAPE

Abuse and violence
Use and misuse
Human shield, rape.

Women and children
Raped, raped to death
Raped in front of spouses
Before parents, siblings and relatives,
Rape, a war tool, they call it.

Taboos, abominations, desecration
Violations, evil, sacrileges
They rape, they rape, they rape,
They maim, kill and dismember
Women and children, victims of war.

Whispers of the Biafran skeleton
The sun rising and setting
Setting to rise
And rising to set no more.

AMMUNITION

Soldiers with poor ammunitions
Civilians, recruited with machetes
Tender and young
Armatures, inexperienced
Fighting to defend and secure.

Hungered, troubled, thirsted, bothered
Faith held o, hope glittered
Strength failed, weapons died
There were no ammunitions.

Numbers outnumbered
Might, federal out-mighted
Weapons, crude and ancient
Zeal was there, passion too was,
Fighting with mere courage.

The sun of East
East of the wise,
Wise men following stars
Stars among births.

HUNGER

The land became barren
As bombs dropped and dropped
Farms got wiped off
As grenades exploded,
Foods were gone
Livestock dead,
Hunger increased.

Men ate rats and lizards
There were no salt
Water was scarce
As rivers and streams dried
Vegetations stunted and dwindled.

Money was useless
Children were starved
Women raped and stripped
Men captured, abducted
Hunger killed millions.

The sun is rising, setting and rising
I hear it whisper, in these rays.

TRENCHES

Trenches were there
Dug by soldiers, hungry and angry
Sand parapet, protecting nothing.

Retreat, surrender
Reinforcement, casualties
Trenches knew blood,
Blood upon blood
Sorrow, without measure.

They dug with their might
They dug with their blood
They fought with their soul
They won with their spirit,
They lost to hate, tribalism, sabotage.

But the sun rises
It rises to set no more
Wise men from the east
Stars guiding the shepherds.

UNIFORM

Many wore uniforms
Many wore mufti
Yet they knew themselves
Just with that badge
That badge of the rising sun.

Uniform amidst hunger
Uniform against hate
Uniform warding off intimidation
They wore, they did not wear
But they fought against odds
Contrary with the evens
The evens that deterred them.

I hear these whispers
Whispers if the Biafran skeleton
Skulls whispering
Ghosts haunting
They are restless
Blood speaking, avenging, very vengeful.

MARGINALIZATION

You fought marginalization
You wanted equity
You reached out for equity
So, you battled segregation.

You were sidetracked
You were made the black sheep
You were double-crossed
So, you went for defense.

Marginalization even from your wealth
Your oil was sold and bought
Your land acquired and reshuffled
Yet, you were not aware.

They marginalized you to the extreme
You were pushed to the wall
You were suffocating
So, you had no option.

Listen to the whispers
These whispers whistle
They wake the dead.

DEATHS

Young women became widows
And children became fatherless,
Many turned orphans
The aged became childless
Because there were deaths.

Deaths, deaths, deaths
Death too climbed, escalated
Corpses littered, decaying and decomposing
Vultures married, partied and banqueted
Skeletons of millions everywhere.

Dreams and hopes, futures
Aspirations and ambitions, numerous
Worlds, worlds, cloudy and moody
Fate, misty and cloudy.

Yet listen, for I hear
Yes, I hear whispers
Whispers of them
Then, the Biafran skeleton
They whisper and whistle
Yes, they are not at rest.

BRIDGE

There were not much bridges
Some were local and poor
That could link, not motorable
Yet were blown off
Blown off, to get them trapped
So that they die like rats.

Bridges were blown off
Sinking enemies, drowning foes
But I say I hear whispers.

Now bridges built, armature and temporary
Woods, bamboos, whatever
But humans, animals, loads, passed.

Passed, passed to nowhere maybe
For some still died, never reached
Lo, look, listen and hear
I hear whispers of them all.

Whispers of the Biafran skeleton
It haunts, it taunts, it worries.

REFINERY

Refineries were built
Built to help and augment
Local manpower, steady strength
Fighting tooth and nail
Not minding strange forces.

Brains, spirits, zeal, trust
Enthusiasm, willingness, passion
Patriotism, loyalty, unity, togetherness
Conquest and victory at sight
Refinery to set up a young nation.

Feeding plant, feeder station
Crude, energizing crude people
Motivating a losing camp
Yet victory songs are heard.

These whispers transpire and triumph
They linger longer than necessary
Because ears are itchy
Eyes are open, tongues confess
That Biafra was a child.

WAR MUSEUM

Skulls and skeletons
Guns and cars
Bombs and grenades
Maps and uniforms
In war museums.

They are Biafrans, great and small
They hoped for Biafra
They beckoned for freedom
They were tired of intimidation
So, they fought in defense of their freedom.

These museums, poor or rich
They are significant and symbolic
They are great and mighty
Call it humiliation or destruction
These museums house dreams.

I hear whispers of these dreams
They whisper of freedom and equality
They still whisper for equity and justice.

EVACUATION

Poor evacuation
Unhealthy movements
Babies, children, pregnant women
Men and children,
Little or no salvage.

Some died, trekking
Some gave up, ferrying
Some lost, transporting
Evacuation, a mockery of safety.

But hark, these tidings
Tidings of tears and joy
News, news of hope and war
Traumas amidst dramas
Listen, I hear whispers.

Whispers of skeletons
Skeletons of Biafra
Biafrans, heroes and heroines
They whisper, yes they whisper.

ONE MAN ONE BULLET

One man, one bullet
They chanted, they sang
Yes, they did, they actually did.

Things were terrible
Terribly bad, to that point
No matter the shellings
Despite the bombings
They took solace in that,
One man, one bullet
Because they had few or none.

It meant thorough carefulness
You dare not shoot except at sight
You shoot moving enemies
The noise notwithstanding.

Yes, I still hear them whisper
They are whispering and murmuring
Whispers of the Biafran skeleton
Voices unknown, unseen, unhindered.

ABDUCTION

Many were abducted
Taken to strange lands
There, they were married off
For the ones lucky enough
Some were violated grossly
Some, raped repeatedly.

There, they were penetrated
Front and back, back and front
By not one, two of three men
But by as many as possible.

The intimidation was terrible
Old and young, young and old
Males and females, girls and boys
Sex slaves, sex objects, not even prostitution.

Hear now the whispers
Hear them loud and clear
Whispers so horrifying
Whispers of innocence.

LOOTS

The loots were great
Looting of all kinds
Looters became rich.

Men in the field, dying
Fighting with bare feet and hands
Scorpions at home, looting.

Looting beyond imagination
Setting up and settling themselves
While brave men lose.

Yes, I still hear them whisper
These whispers are tormenting
They torture the peaceful
And annoy the devastated.

I hear whispers, whispers of the Biafran skeleton
Murmurs, shouting, pleadings
Prayers, noises, alarms, war songs,
Listen, I hear, I hear still
I hope they end in praise.

BLOCKADE

Information was barred, barred and blocked
Waves and frequencies shut down
The Media was endangered
Wrong and inaccurate ones found way.

Blackout and darkness
Scarcity, lack, want and need
Deliberate targets to wipe off
Blockades, roadblocks and barricades.

Foreign bodies, strange organizations
Helps and aids, gone and lost
A people struggling to breathe.

Still hear the whispers
They whisper, they whistle
They wrestle to be heard
Yes, I hear them loud and clear
These whispering skeletons are frightening.

THINGS FELL APART

Yes indeed, things fell apart
When the seat was hotter than fire
Some threw in the towel
Some paid, some bribed.

A lot of sabotage and camouflage
Infiltration and saboteurs
 Cowards and cowardice
Yet, in the face of bravery.

Strong men fought gods
They conquered their shrines
And burnt them down
Only that they were murdered.

Things fell apart, yes it did
But it might not have fallen
It fell because there were no options.

But listen clearly, I still hear them whisper
The whisperings from Biafran skeleton.

CAPTURED

There were captured soldiers
Soldiers who should not have been captured
They became prisoners of war
They laboured, they suffered
Some relayed vital information.

The worst you can be is a captured soldier
All the hate and bitterness will be on you.

Some buried alive
Some beheaded,
Some dismembered
Some burnt.

Captured for fun, captured to toss around
Captured soldiers, a show of power
A display of strength.

Hear still the whispers
The whispers of this great skeleton,
Whispering in deaf ears.

ENEMY

Some unknown, unseen, unheard
Someone alien, strange, foreign
Someone, different, unique, outstanding
In a twinkle, turns an enemy.

No personal offense, no grudge
Just an order from above
An order to humiliate, kill and murder
An order to conquer, bury and subdue
Any one becomes an instant enemy.

Enemy troops, enemy battalion, enemy territory
Enemy, just like that
Nothing more, nothing less
Victory is the track
History is the aim,
Conquest, by all means.

Listen though, these whispers are loud
You dare not silence them
They whisper and whisper still
Listen, hear, tell the story.

TRIBALISM

Tongues and tribes, colours and races
Religions and cultures, dreams and hopes
All fought, all fighting.

Tribalism, nepotism, favouritism
Fanaticism, hate, bigotry, betrayals
Fans and shafts of greed
Greedy lords and selfish tycoons,
Blowing bugles of war
And luring palatable lust,
Killing the unborn.

You can still hear those whispers
Whispers beyond the world
Worlds of fame, worlds of greed
Worlds of politics and religion.

Oh, really I hear, I hear, I hear
Whispers of the Biafran skeleton
Ages gone, lives lived
Yet, they whisper.

NO VICTOR

They lied, there was a victor
The victor lied, he vanquished
When justice is dead
There was a victor
When equity is killed
There was a vanquisher.

No victor; big lie
A deceiver deceiving,
An obvious deceit.

Celebrated, crowned, wined and dined
In character, words and deeds
In omens, behaviors
Patterns and tactics
In speculations, specifications and segregations
The Victor is glaring, bold and callous.

The victor sings and merries
Pretending to be deaf and dumb
Blind to the whispers of the Biafran skeleton
But the skeletons still whisper aloud.

NO VANQUISHED

There was a vanquished
The vanquished knows himself
He hides it not
He says it loud
In his cravings and pleadings
In his protests, and prayers
In his submissions and petitions
The vanquished, elaborates it all.

Poisoned land, porous farms
Sidetracked positions, withdrawn offices
Scraped portfolios, burnt files
The vanquished knows himself.

No vanquished; big lie
There was a vanquished and a vanquisher
Both know themselves
Both know each other
They hide it not, though they pretend.

Both hear whispers
The victor hears, the vanquished hears
And they know these are whispers from the Biafran skeleton.

NO VICTOR NO VANQUISHED

No victor, no vanquished
The victor celebrates
No victor, no vanquished
The vanquished, laments.

No victor, no vanquished
Yet no peace, no love, no unity
No victor, no vanquished
Yet no progress, no change
Both hear whispers.

No victor, no vanquished
Look, blood flowing
No victor, no vanquished
Look, corpses littered,
No victor, no vanquished
See them shooting and bombing
Burning and killing,
Maiming and raping.

No victor, no vanquished
White lie, white lie, lie and deceit.

Listen and hear, hear whispers
Whispers of the Biafran skeleton.

FREEDOM

Freedom is costly, costlier than gold
But slavery is cheaper, cheaper than mud.

Yokes are heavy, heavier than the neck
Brass are cursed, upon the shoulders.

Wear not slavery, wear not shield
If they are against freedom.

Freedom is rich, richer than money
Courage is great, greater than barns.

Fight for freedom, retain your freedom
Fight for freedom, maintain your freedom.

Hatred is a witch, lust is a wizard
Marginalization is a beast, segregation is a monster.

Hear then the whispers, skeletons, skeletons
They whisper, they whisper
They whisper freedom and love
They long for unity and emancipation.

WAR SONGS

Rhythms, melodies and gyrations
Words, songs and hymns
All, some soldiers could get.

Morale, low at a point
Morale, high at the other point
Morale, lost and gone
Yet, the fight is on.

War songs of victory
War songs for victory
War songs of hope
War songs for hope,
Echoes, echoes, chants and chants
Men of little support.

Whispers I hear, whispers I hear
Whispers of peace, whispers of love
Whispers of unity, whispers of freedom
Hear, heed, hearken, listen
I hear them, whispers from the Biafran skeleton.

DESTRUCTION

Homes gone, houses gone
Roads bombed, schools bombed
Markets, hospitals, bombs everywhere
Wreckages, absurd scenes
Nowhere is free nor fair.

Victims of war, casualties
Poor and rich, great and small
Tall and short, young and old
Destruction beyond reasons.

Communications in extinctions
Relationships in danger
Families, bereaved
Amidst these, I hear whispers.

Biafran skeleton, parading
Whispering to the world at large
Calling for freedom, calling for justice.

GENOCIDE

Millions died untimely
Intentional starvation
Deprivation of salt and water
Closure, blockade, negligence
Millions, swept under carpet.

Innocent children, weak women
Tortures and torments, pains and pangs
Killings and hangings, severances
Genocide, a whooping hatred.

Vultures feasted, maggots dined
Dust and sand, buried the chosen
Genocide, homicide, suicide.

I am hearing whispers
These whispers are not ordinary,
They come from the Biafran skeleton.

MASS GRAVES

Numerous graves, here and there
For those honourably buried
Mass graves across
Men and women in hundreds
Children in their numbers
Innocence, strength, hopes, all gone.

Mass graves abound
Voices of Biafrans
Bodies of them all
Buried like flies,
Earth swallowed them in numbers.

These mass graves whisper
They whisper and call names
They bleed and shout
They murmur and debate
They are truly unhappy.

Whispering graves, whispering land
Museums that whisper
Hear them, whispering.

CONSCRIPTION

For those unwilling to join
For those afraid to fight
For those unhappy to die
For those innocent to bomb
For those tender to kill
I hear them whispering.

Conscripted, forced and laboured
Embraced, unwillingly and unhappily
Fielded wrongly and intentionally
These ones still whisper.

The ones taken from their homes
The ones taken from their mothers
The ones hidden in the bushes
The ones chased far away
They are still whispering.

I hear them all, they whisper
They whisper Biafra, Biafra
They cry amidst these whispers.

POWER TUSSLE

Terrible power pushing terrible men
Forcing them to kill
Horrible quest luring them all
Compelling them to not keep alive.

Power tussle, they fling lives
Lives of common men
They bomb, they terrorize
They blow up communities
These give them joy
And retain their influence.

Hear them, the whispers
The whispers increase
Daily, weekly, annually.

O dear whispers
Whispers of freedom
Whispers for freedom
Whispering beyond war.

BUSINESS

Of the business that suffered
And the ones that thrived,
Of the moguls that manipulated
And the figures that maneuvered
Businesses and drafts
Politics and plans
Destroying futures, futures unborn.

Arms deals, boomed
For the might that conquered
Arms deals won
For the might that fought
Arms deals swollen
For the might that tested
Tested poor Biafra,
Biafra, fighting with zeal.

Listen, listen attentively
I still hear those whispers
These whispers are harder
They are intense and farther.

TRAPS

There were traps
Traps within and without
Locally and nationally
They aimed at Biafra.

Traps in all forms
Focused on wiping off
Wide, large, huge and gigantic
Tender Biafra, raw and unfed
Fighting and advancing with hope.

Mighty enemy with support
Strong for with recognition
Looming, booming, blossoming
Only to swallow Biafra
But she stood, until she fell.

Hear it again, there is a whisper
Whispers from a whisperer
Whispering to be heard
The whispers of pain.

DEFENSE

Biafra never went to war
She was at home
They brought war to her
So, she defended herself.

She was bruised and battered
Wounded and flogged
She was messed up and mesmerized
Yet she defended herself.

Her territory was invaded
Her colony, captured
Her might, fell
Yet she defended herself.

She was a victor
Yet, the vanquished
Although no victor, no vanquished
She fought hard to live.

I hear her, whisper
I hear her, whispering
She whispers hard
Whispering for emancipation.

LOST

There were many, lost
Lost in transit
Old and young
They were lost.

These ones found themselves elsewhere
Running from bombs and attacks,
They lost their way
Till date, they never returned.

They have sojourned in foreign lands
They became them automatically.

These ones, no more news from them
Families forgotten, relatives unknown
Generations, begetting and forgetting.

Listen, they whisper still
Their souls abound in wonder
As their spirits wander,
Hear, I can hear them
Whispering home is beyond.

OJUKWU

When you fought
Things were not this bad
When you "rebelled"
It was not this terrible
Now we understand
Now we see,
Now we comprehend
Why you "went" to war.

Giant, you were
Hero, you are
Hero, the hero
The true hero in essence
Now, we know better.

Only you pulled the trigger
You stopped a coup, rendered it immobile
You defended your people
You shook the world
Amidst trials and tribulations.

I can hear whispers
Whispers of pride.

DAD

You trekked from home to camp
In the middle of the night
You enlisted in the army
To fight for your fatherland.

You wanted freedom
And still want freedom,
You loved peace
And still love peace
You preferred justice
And still prefer justice
You preached equity
And still preach equity,
Dad, you fought not in vain.

Many flew, many hid, many ran
Many wounded, many lost, many died
But you returned hale and hearty
Happy, proud, sane and stronger.

I can hear you whisper
Whispering for peace and justice
Whispering for unity and equity
Those whispers are strong.

AMALGAMATION

Some were aware
Some were not aware
And some were taken unawares.

Different people can live in peace
But they must first agree,
There is a great power in diversity
There, could be unity,
If and only if they decide to stay.

Forces can scatter
Powers can destroy
Same forces can gather
Same powers can build
Differences and similarities make or mar.

Diversities whisper, differences whisper
Similarities whisper, they all are whispering
Hear them whisper, I hear them too.

TONGUES AND TRIBES

They were many
Many of different tongues and tribes
The Igbos, Itsekiris, Ijaws, Efiks, Idomas, Ikweres,
Calabaris, Ogonis, Urhobos, and others.

They were the Biafrans
They had one dream,
Until they were struck.

These tongues and tribes scattered
They littered across everywhere
Fighting, hating and killing each other.

They were used and abused
They were misused and dumped
They were traded and mortgaged.

They never wanted it so
But powers descended on them
And planted great enmity.

Now, they hear whispers
And they whisper too.

EXILE

Many went on exile
And died there,
Some returned and died here.

The warlord was exiled
Though he returned
And died here.

If he had been captured alive
Who knew the fate that would have befallen him?

Thank God he left
He left for safety
As advised,
Till date, he lives
He lives in history,
No wonder his name is in the encyclopedia.

That alone whispers, yes it does
Whispers from exile and the exiled
I hear them even now
They whisper for emancipation.

REFUGEES

Millions of refugees
Running helter-skelter
Searching for safety
Looking for food,
They became homeless
Homeless in their fatherland.

They starved, they hungered
They thirsted, they longed
They were stranded and helpless
They were hopeless and lifeless.

Women abandoned their children
Fathers abandoned their households
It was survival of the fittest.

Nothing was sweet, life was bitter
They wangled, wobbled, joggled amidst jungles
They wandered and wondered
They ran, crawled, trekked and slept
Under the sun, in the rains, cold and heat
They suffered, they died in their numbers
I hear them, Oh yes
I hear them whispering.

MONEY

The Biafran money was real
True currency with value,
It had pride and prize.

The money was true
A real currency with honour
It was great and bright.

It had strength and prestige
No fake, no loss, no regret
Her currency was hard and current.

Lost now and gone
Forgotten and useless
Yet hear them, whispering.

This currency whispers
It struggles to be heard
Flying in the wind
Spreading like a bird
Oh, I hear it again and again.

BURIAL RITES

And this is for them all
Wherever they may be now
Some dead, some still alive.

These ones, the ones that were declared or rumoured dead
The ones whose burial rites were performed
I mean, they returned alive after the rites.

Dad returned, after rumours of his death
Alexander Madiebo met villagers "burying" him
People ran away when dad returned
Alexander Madiebo, returned same day of his "burial."

There are others too, known and unknown
Some forgotten, some "buried," some mourned
But they returned alive after all these.

This is for them all
Those honoured or not
I hear them whisper,
They whisper clearly aloud
They whisper peace and progress.

BIGHT OF BIAFRA

Maps bore you clear
They could not erase you
Old maps carved you well
You are there plain and bold
The Bight of Biafra.

A land of riches
Oil, yam, rice, vegetable
You boomed and dazzled
Born but miscarried
You were there, your voice echoed.

The Bight of Biafra
A land of golden greatness
Where harmony was melodious
You were troubled and killed
But still you whisper.

Whispers so lingering
Lingering unto the unborn.

SHADOWS

Shadows everywhere
Ghosts, souls, spirits
Clapping, dancing, murmuring
They are praying for peace.

Their peaceful prayers arise
They burn like incense
They smell pleasant.

These bodies decayed and gone
Yet restless and troubled
They are worried of unity
They dare emancipation.

Hear them, Oh hear them
Hear them, over and over
Again and again and again
They whisper, whisper
Whispering for liberation.

SKELETONS

Of these children malnourished
Of these ones shapeless
These ones whose stomachs protruded
Small heads, lean legs, tiny hands
Thin bodies, weak eyes
Pale bones, faint voices
Helpless feet, hopeless faces
Of these terrible lives, I hear.

I hear them still begging
Pleading, appeasing, appealing
Intervening, interceding, meditating
Petitioning, canvassing, charming
Enchanting and speeding.

I hear them whisper
Songs of freedom
Hear them echo;
Redemption song.

LORRIES

Of those lorries
Lorries of corpses
Corpses of your able-bodied men
Men with vigour and life
That were butchered
Butchered just like that.

Yes, of those lorries that brought them
Men killed with impunity
Men whisked away in their prime
Yes, of those lorries
We hear them whisper.

Whispers of innocence
Whispers of loyalty
Whispers of negligence
Whispers of agony
Whispers of wickedness
Whispers of ungodliness
Yes, they whisper
Of how they were dehumanized.

Let all hear these whispers
For the whispers trouble the earth
And pressurize the living.

AHBURI ACCORD

For the Ahburi accord
And its agreement
These whispers wonder,
Whispers sweeping carpets
Turning tables and unseating men.

They stood on Ahburi
They agreed on Ahburi
They announced Ahburi.

For those against it
For those for Ahburi
For those under it
For those beyond Ahburi
For them that scattered it
The agreement that confuses
A complicated vow we know not
Oh, for them all, we hear whispers.

Ahburi whispers, whispers from Ahburi
We still hear those whispers.

AHIARA DECLARATION

Ojukwu, give us gun
Ojukwu, give us gun
Give us gun, Ojukwu
They chanted in unison
Great men ready for battle.

Give us gun, Ojukwu
Ojukwu, give us gun
They all chanted in unison
At the Ahiara Declaration
Little did they really know about war.

They knew not they had none
And that the federal might is unwinnable
Give us gun, Ojukwu
They did not only chant, they fought
They fought and died.

Young men, handsome and healthy
Brave and bold, courageous
Strong, they fought, they did actually.

The Ahiara Declaration
The voice of Biafra
The eagerness and passion
The freedom, liberation and liberty.

An orphan is helpless, powerless
An orphan hopeless, restless

Biafra was an orphan
Helpless, powerless, hopeless and restless
Yet, stronger than many
Fought for months and years
Defended, stood, won and lost
Still undefeated, a spirit.

I hear Biafra, whisper
Whispering to my ears
Disturbing and distorting my peace
A desperate whisper to be born.

INJUSTICE

Senseless killings and murders
Worthless maiming and dismemberment
In a land of ours
In a home of all
A people taken for granted.

Unity on paper, disunity on grounds
Peace on lips, war on realities
Injustice, all nooks and crannies.

Equal rights, the sermon
Black sheep, the service
Qualifications apart
Ignorance on set
Illiteracy, the king
Education, the servant
They all are whispering.

1967-1970

Years of inhumane course
The years men withheld life
Yes, they brewed death.

These years, Biafra suffered
Born and died within same time
Choked, suffocated, strangled
Buried and never was mourned.

These years torment
They haunt and hunt till date
They spread their tentacles
Reaching out to be felt
Shouting and demonstrating
Causing the world to think.

1967-1970 is still whispering
For the pounded flesh and stripped flowers
They whisper, Oh I hear them.

MILITARY HOSPITALS

Schools turned hospitals
Schools became camps
Military hospitals and refugee camps
Accepting and treating victims
Housing and sheltering casualties.

These hospitals buried much
Many, mass graves.
Hunger, drugs, whatever.

Military hospitals, helped
They did their best
With their might and in their might
They catered treated, cured.

War is a beast
The masses die
The soldiers die
The power holders gamble.

But I hear all the whispers
Whispers of the Biafran skeleton
Buried in the world beyond
Yet, wouldn't rest
Hear him, whisper.

GREED

Greed, beyond imagination
Greediness, to a fault
Greedy, dubious
Bitter, crude, archaic
Backward, selfish
Greediness, cause of war.

Selfish leaders everywhere
Dominating and domineering
Autocratic,
Lustful, vengeful, hateful
Always abusive, careless
Reluctant, nonchalant
Non remorseful, ungodly
All those killed Biafrans.

Biafra, tender and green
Futuristic and friendly
Vision for liberty
Movement for liberation
But captured, condemned, slaughtered.

Yet Biafra whispers
Whispering constantly and continuously
Whispering and calling.

VITAL POSITIONS

In a land of professed unity
And pledged oneness
Vital positions go to a clique
Even ignorant and illiterate ones.

Qualified people lose out
Interested fellows; flushed out
These posts reserved for families
Retired and old ones
Men of not much integrity
They get called back
They get reemployed
But the young and deserving men lose,
Yes, they lose steadily.

A particular tribe, rules
A specific people leads
A concentrated tongue, sings
A certain religion, terrorizes.

When you lead and order
Forcing others to follow
Even when they are better
When you hurt and wound
Compelling others to swallow trash
Even when they can retaliate,
When you take your fill
And starve others
Never expect their silence forever.

I hear therefore, whispers
Whispers, longing and lingering
Wanting to be great
Needing to be heard
These whispers are inborn.

TODAY

Till date, you kill them
Until now, you persecuted them
Hitherto, you enslaved them.

These voices sing loud
As they die, they pray
They curse and cry
They wail and weep
They call on gods
They lay before God
They utter mysteries.

Hear them, hear them now
Our ears are deaf
Our lips are dumb
Our legs are lame
Our eyes are blind
Our hands are tied
Yet, they whisper louder.

Nothing is permanent
No condition lasts forever
These tears pile up
These decompositions swell
They heap, they tower, they smell
Towering to the heavens.

Whispers of the Biafran skeleton
Tired, faint, weak and poor
Yet, it would not stop whispering.

PATRIOTISM

Patriotism is dead
Unionism is gone
Solidarity is buried
One you, one me, one us
That was then
One us is gone, really gone.

Soldiers are no more interested
Their morale is very low
Infiltrated and sabotaged
Frustrated and court marshalled
They die in their numbers.

They even know, they murmur
They know they are being used
They feel it, they feel it
They see it in the air
Their people sacrifice them.

Young widows, fatherless unborn
Unmarried spinsters, dead heroes.

The skeleton mocks, it laughs
The skeleton mimics, it initiates
Amidst pain and penury
Amidst sorrows and tears
Amidst blood and flesh.

LOSSES

Listen to old women now
Those who survived the war
Hear them recount their losses
Jewels, wrappers
Boxes, books, and monies
They ran leaving some
Some were burnt
Some destroyed by termites.

Hear them tell stories
Stories of war planes
Stories of bombings
Of how they hid their children
Especially male children
Hidden against conscription
And female children
Hidden against rape.

Losses, losses upon losses
Sighings, angers, regrets
Wishes, and prayers
As they forbid anymore war.

Upon that I hear whispers
Whispers of this skeleton
Terrifying, frowning and freezing
Whispers from the Biafran skeleton.

AMBUSHED

For the soldiers advancing
For the ones retreating
For the soldiers reinforcing
For the ones surrendering,
They fought their best.

Waylaid and ambushed
Targeted and bombed
Bought or sold, tricked or pranked
Sabotaged or camouflaged
They fought, they really did.

Incentives, poor and low
Entitlements, nowhere, none
A people fighting for pride
A group out for their name
A land precious and dare
So united and great
So keen and dedicated
Committed and real
But betrayed and sold out.

Biafra whispers, the skeleton
Hear, Oh hear, hear
The whispers are real
They are groaning.

FRUSTRATIONS

Poverty was there
Abandonment blew
Rejection and dejection
Frustrations ruled your tent.

Efforts were great
Great to conquer
Enemies were large
Large, large, just to murder.

You tried holding on
You pushed front and back
You stood your grounds
You made history
But you were frustrated.

Alone and alone
Lonely and bored
Powerless and weaponless
Yet focused to win.

You win, for attempting
You won for fighting
You won for letting go
You could not have continued.

As you lay in those graves
Graves, big and small
As deceived in those bushes

Bushes, thick and thin
As you trained in spirit
So, you whisper to us.

We hear, yes, we do
We hear still them
These whispers are windy
They possess, they lift.

THE STRUGGLE

Oh yes, the struggle
The struggle is huge
It towered to the Everest
And rooted to the abyss
Sideways, it stretches.

Daily, it refreshes
Bleeds hot and red
Bites new and yonder
The struggle is indeed real.

A prayer to let go
The head rears in gears
A wish to be gone
The tail tangles
This struggle whispers;
I am the Biafran skeleton.

BIAFRA

I want freedom
Give me liberty
I want emancipation
Give me Justice
I want peace
Give me equity
Otherwise I shall not rest.

You cannot silence me
You cannot kill me
I am a skeleton
I am invisible
I am unknown
I am alive
I walk, I run, I feed
I am Biafra
Let me be.

I whisper, I knock
I knock, I whisper
I patrol and parade
I am restless
For you did me evil.

My plea is simple
Let me live, let me live
My prayer is just
Let me exist.

ATROCITIES

Pregnant women were raped
Raped to death
Virgins were severed
Severed underneath
Warriors were hanged
Hanged upside down
Atrocities upon atrocities.

Foetuses were bared
Bared for vultures
Wombs were cut
Cut for maggots,
Intestines were split
Split for dirts
Throats were slit
Slit for dusts
Split and slit for fun
Atrocities, atrocities, against mankind.

Hear them whispering
Whispering and whistling
See them in whirlwinds
Whirlwinds of violence
They are restless
Pacing and panting
Wanting to be free
Oh, hear them whisper.

MILLIONS OF BIAFRANS

In thirty months
Millions of Biafrans died,
The world did not mourn.

In thirty months
Millions of Biafrans decayed
The world was silent.

In thirty months
Millions of Biafrans decomposed
The world did not know.

In thirty months
Millions of Biafrans fought
They fought hunger and starvation
They fought blockade and kwashiorkor
They struggled, they wrestled
They bowed, they gave up
Yes, in thirty months
The world blinked not an eye.

But till date, they whisper
Those millions whisper
They move up and down
Loitering in the spiritual realm
They whisper nothing but freedom.

LEADERSHIP

Sometimes, leaders do harm
They care not for the masses,
They institute laws for themselves
And ordain ordinances to safeguard them.

They thwart rules
And flout stipulations,
They ruin norms
And abuse power
They violate rule of law
And kill natural conscience.

They break hedges and edges
They lay siege
And raze tents
They do whatever that sustains them.

Wars are avoidable
Violence can be curtailed
Humiliation, exploitation, violation
All these can be stopped
But leadership builds ladders for them.

Education dwindles, civilization kills
Politics, torments
Religion traumatizes
Because they want perpetual power.

But listen and listen well
Hear the Biafran skeleton
The whispers are scary.

FAULTY FOUNDATION

Injustice shoots up
Nothing is by merit anymore,
Bribery and corruption, siblings and offsprings.

Merit, dead and gone
Trust, lost long ago
Truth, whitewashed
Decency, eroded
Moral decadence,
A faulty foundation.

Fairness and freeness
None buys them,
Integrity and loyalty
None commissions them
Dedication and diligence
None applauds them,
A faulty foundation.

On that faulty foundation
Biafra beckons and whispers
Whispering, crying, weeping
Forbearing, to be freed.

AGUIYI IRONSI

He was an Igbo man
He was a general
So, he needed to die.

His, was a cross-country
He was towed round and around
Until he gave up.

A general in the army
A warrior, a hero
A voice, an iroko.

His spirit still whispers
He whispers for rest
For freedom, for justice
Yes, Aguiyi whispers.

All the dead, those killed by that war
The Nigeria civil war
The Biafran revolution
Those murdered within the then Eastern states
Buried, unburied, seen, unseen
Known, unknown, great, small
Civilians, soldiers, all Biafrans
They whisper, I can hear them,
Yes, I hear them.

This evil is still on
These killings still grow
Stop! Stop!! Stop!!!
Let my people be free.

NGOZI OLIVIA OSUOHA is a Nigerian poet/writer/thinker. A graduate of Estate Management with experience in Banking and Broadcasting.

She has published five poetry books and co-authored one (with Amos O. Ojwang').

She has featured in more than forty international anthologies and also has published over two hundred and fifty poems/articles in over twenty countries.

Many of her poems have been translated and published into other languages, including Spanish, Romanian, Khloe, Farsi, and Arabic, among others.

She has won many awards; she is a one time BEST OF THE NET NOMINEE, and she has numerous words on marble.

www.ingramcontent.com/pod-product-compliance
Lightning Source LLC
Chambersburg PA
CBHW020145130526
44591CB00030B/233